MY COLOUR BOOK OF
GEOGRAPHY

A bright, easy-to-read introduction to the world we live in

KEAY

KEAY

ELSA JANE WERNER

Illustrated by Cornelius De Witt

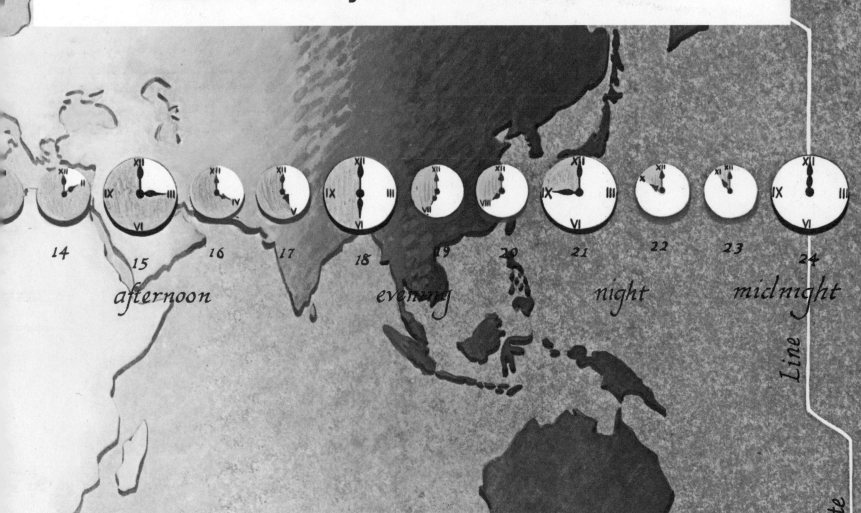

14 15 16 17 18 19 20 21 22 23 24

afternoon   evening   night   midnight

International   Date   Line

HAMLYN

LONDON·NEW YORK·SYDNEY·TORONTO

This is our earth as seen from space. The earth is a huge globe-shaped mass of rock and vapour spinning in space. It is one of the planets which revolve around the sun, and is a part of the solar system. Two-thirds of the earth's surface is covered with the waters of the great seas and oceans. The remaining area of dry land is divided into the continents.

First published 1969
Second impression 1970
Published 1969 by The Hamlyn Publishing Group Limited
London · New York · Sydney · Toronto
Hamlyn House, Feltham, Middlesex, England.
for Golden Pleasure Books Limited
© Copyright by Western Publishing Company Incorporated 1952, 1964
Printed in Czechoslovakia by TSNP, Martin.
ISBN 0 601 07340 1

THE CONTINENTS

The earth's great bodies of land are the continents. The continents have been named Asia, Europe, Africa, North America, South America, Australia and Antarctica.

Around them the oceans of water flow together — the Atlantic, Pacific, Arctic, Antarctic and Indian Oceans. Each of the three great oceans — the Atlantic, the Pacific and the Indian — is much bigger than any of the continents. In fact, all the land on earth put together would not cover the entire surface of the vast Pacific Ocean.

In Turkey the young people are taking over modern European ways in dress and manners.

Old and new methods of agriculture meet in Asia Minor.

The hot climate of India means that a good deal of life is spent out-of-doors.

In the high Himalayas people exchange goods by barter instead of buying and selling.

Some Arab States have traditional customs, such as veils for women.

THIS IS ASIA

Asia is the largest of the continents. It goes halfway up and down the earth and a third of the way around. It is bigger than North America and South America put together. It has many more people than any other continent. It has the world's highest mountain peak, Mt. Everest, in the Himalayas. And it has the world's lowest dry land, near the Dead Sea between Israel and Jordan.

Asia has some of the world's oldest nations, like the high tableland of Tibet, which China now rules. And it has some of the newest self-ruling nations in the Southeast.

ARCTIC OCEAN

In vast wooded stretches of Siberia a few people live in villages, growing grain and seeds for oil.

Manchuria is the industrial heart of Asia. Here there are great factories.

People of China have adopted some Western ways, but there is still Oriental colour in their lives.

Many races mingle in the seaports of Southern Asia.

Asia has two huge deserts, the Arabian and Gobi deserts, where nomads live. It has thick, not jungles in the Malay Peninsula, and great stretches of cold, windswept plains in Siberia. It has wild hill country in India and Afghanistan, and thickly settled farmlands in India and China, where great rivers rise and flood the low parts of the country every year.

Asia still has some of the world's richest rulers, with huge palaces and treasures of gold and jewels. And it has millions of the world's poorest people, who seldom have enough to eat, or a chance to go to school.

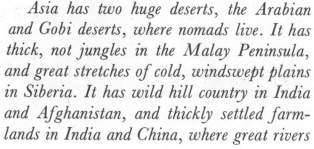

BARENT

ICELAND

ATLANTIC OCEAN

NORTH SEA

WH SE

SWEDEN

FINLAND

BALTIC SEA

SCOTLAND

NORTHERN IRELAND

GREAT BRITAIN

EIRE

WALES

ENGLAND

DENMARK

POLAND

SOVIET

English Channel

BELGIUM

GERMANY

Seine R.

Rhine R.

FRANCE

Loire R.

CZECHO-SLOVAKIA

Danube R.

Rhone R.

SWITZERLAND

AUSTRIA

CARPATHIAN MTS.

HUNGARY

Po R.

RUMANIA

PYRENEES MTS.

Danube R.

PORTUGAL

SPAIN

ITALY

ADRIATIC SEA

YUGOSLAVIA

BULGARIA

Dn

Balearic Islands

CORSICA

APENNINE MTS.

SARDINIA

ALBANIA

TURKEY

GREECE

AEGEAN SEA

MEDITERRANEAN SEA

SICILY

THIS IS EUROPE

Europe is a small continent. It is broken up by many high hills and mountains, curving rivers, and rough coastline. It is also broken up into many countries, some large like the Soviet Union, and some very small like Belgium. These have different languages and governments, different ways of doing things. And they have had many wars among themselves. But they have much in common.

The same low plains stretch across France and the low countries of Belgium, the Netherlands, and Denmark. These plains cross northern Germany and Poland to the almost endless lowlands of Russia. Most of the low plains are rich farmlands. Europe is so crowded with people that most farms are small. But the farmers work very hard on them and grow many different fruits and vegetables, grains, and even fields of flowers to sell.

There are many beautiful mountains in Europe. The Alps spread out from Switzerland into France, Germany, Austria, and Italy. Most of the land in the peninsulas of Greece, Spain, and Norway is mountainous. So all these regions have more forests and pastures for flocks and herds than large farms and cities.

In many of the mountainous countries there are swift rivers, which are used for making electric power and for lumbering. There are slow, winding streams in the flatter lands, and these are good highways for boats to travel on, carrying goods.

Europe is a very crowded continent. It has many more people for its size than any other continent. It has many large cities, humming with busy factories. These factories make all sorts of goods, from toys and tiny watches to huge machines.

Almost every one of the countries of Europe has something it makes or grows especially well, which it sends out to sell in many other lands. Some countries are famous for fruits, some for cereals, some for raising fine animals. Others are famous for the products of their factories. The map on this page shows just a few of the many different things produced by the people of Europe.

The flat "low countries" of Northern Europe have many dairy farms.

Fields of flowers in the Netherlands grow on land lower than the sea. Great walls called dykes hold the waters back.

France has many vineyards growing grapes for wine.

Gathering cork gives these men of Spain their living.

Europe has many large cities where thousands of people work in factories, making goods and machines to be sold around the world.

EUROPE

ATLANTIC OCEAN

NORTH SEA

MEDITERRANEAN SEA

The hills of Italy have many olive groves.

Sweden has many hydro-electric plants built along rushing mountain streams.

Lumbering is important in Northern Europe, from Norway across to Russia.

Except for Russia's collective farms, most of Eastern Europe has little farm machinery.

The countries of South-eastern Europe raise tobacco, along with other crops.

Here is one of the busy port cities along the shores of the Mediterranean Sea.

Threshing of grain is still done by old-fashioned methods in Greece.

North Africa has busy Arab towns.

There are rubber plantations in African jungles.

Casablanca

SAHARA

DESERT

GHANA

SOUTH ATLANTIC OCEAN

Cape

THIS IS AFRICA

On the continent of Africa there is no cold winter. The warmest lands on earth are near the imaginary line, the Equator, that runs around the middle of the earth. This line runs across the greenest part of Africa on the map. (You can find the Equator just inside the back of the book, too).

Near the Equator there is hot sunshine. There is lots of rain. Plants grow quickly. Forests are thick. More bright-coloured birds and wild animals live there than people. People who live in the rain forests hunt wild animals and cut down trees to grow some crops.

To the north and south of the rain forests are open grasslands. Across the widest part of the continent, farther north, stretches a great dry desert. There is a desert in the south, too. Almost no rain falls in these deserts. So few plants grow that people who live there must wander to feed their animals — and themselves.

Africa has some high and beautiful mountains. It has some large lakes. It has two of the

Lake Victoria is one of the world's largest lakes.

worlds longest rivers — the Nile and the Congo.

Africa has some of the world's oldest cities, as well as fastgrowing new cities. It has mines, factories and farms. And Africa has many different peoples.

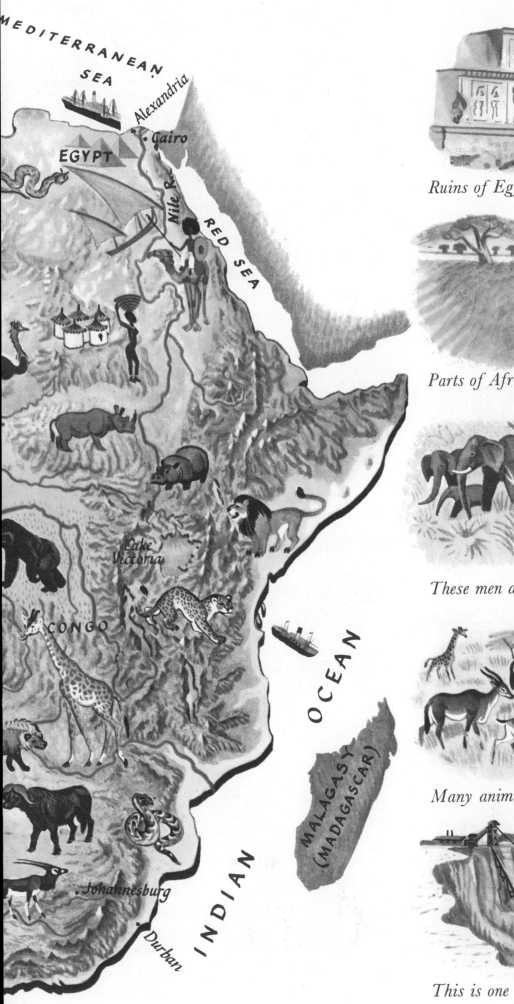

Ruins of Egypt's ancient temples may still be seen.

Parts of Africa have prosperous farms. On this one peanuts are grown.

These men and animals are at home in the jungle.

Many animals use the same water holes together.

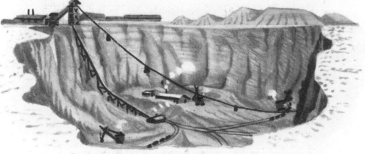

This is one of South Africa's rich diamond mines.

THIS IS SOUTH AMERICA

South America is an uncrowded continent. Along the west coast the world's largest chain of mountains, the Andes, runs all the way from the north to the rocky southern tip of the continent. Some fine cities have been built high in these mountains. But there is still much wild pasture land. And there are great forests of valuable woods on the mountain slopes, and plantations of coffee.

The mountains have riches under the surface, too. Copper, gold, silver, tin and other minerals lie in the rocks, ready to be dug out.

Oil wells in this lake produce great wealth in the South American country of Venezuela.

Copper and silver are smelted into bars to be shipped to many lands.

Uruguay and Argentina, two south-eastern lands, have great cattle herds.

Tobacco is grown on large plantations.

Some Indians still use old-fashioned methods of "cooking" raw rubber.

14

SOUTH AMERICA

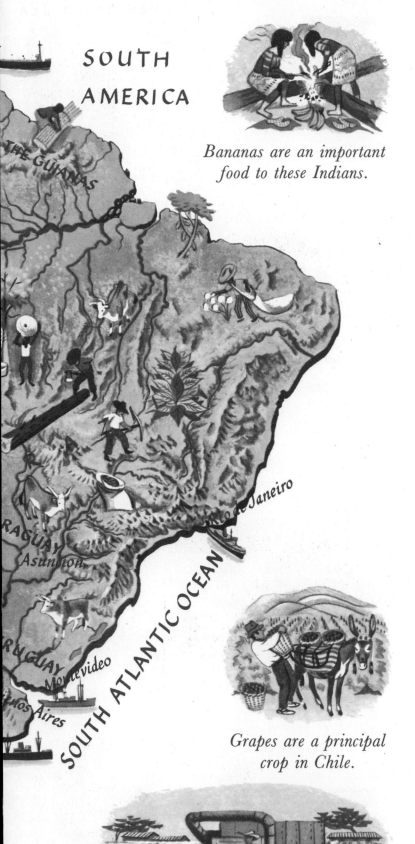

Bananas are an important food to these Indians.

Grapes are a principal crop in Chile.

Cotton is grown in Brazil, South America's largest country.

Coffee beans are one of South America's most important harvests.

The southern lands grow cereals in very large fields.

There are huge, hot, damp forests in the great valleys of the Amazon and Orinoco Rivers. Hundreds of smaller rivers flow into each one of these great ones. And all through those steaming river forests scattered tribal Indians live. Some gather rubber and cacao (cocoa) beans and bananas for traders to ship away.

South America also has great plains. On some, called the pampas, cattle graze. Wheat and grapes and many other farm crops are grown. But there is little crowding. There is space to spare.

This space and the richness of the country have drawn people from many parts of Europe. But it was Spaniards who conquered South America's rich Indian tribes hundreds of years ago. It was Spanish settlers who built up most of the new countries. So most of the cities still have a Spanish look. And Spanish is still spoken in every country but one. Portuguese is spoken in Brazil.

15

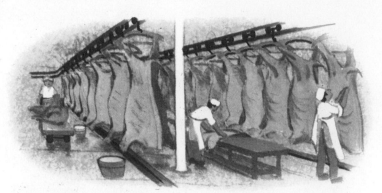

Meat packing is an important industry in South America.

Maté leaves are gathered for tea.

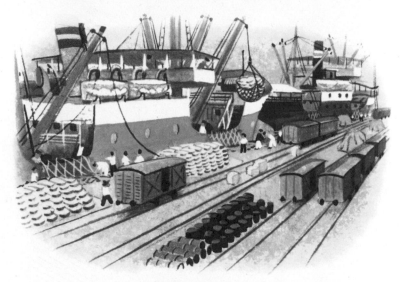

Many sacks of coffee beans are shipped from these busy harbours.

Brazil nuts must be dried in the open air.

Cacao is an important crop.

Many cities in South America have beautiful open squares called plazas.

Llamas carry heavy loads in the Andes.

16

SOUTH AMERICA

Nitrate found in the desert of Chile is used for fertiliser.

On the pampas live the South American cowboys, called gauchos.

Platinum and gold are mined in Columbia in the north.

Rio de Janeiro is one of the most beautiful cities of South America and of the world.

Fountains and tropical plants add charm and splendour to city gardens and estates.

Indian ceremonial dancers wear wonderful costumes.

The sisal plant gives strong fibres.

PACIFIC OCEAN

Mexico City

MEXICO AND CENTRAL AMERICA

The little countries of Central America are like South America in many ways. They were explored and taken over by men from Spain, long ago. But many of their people are Indians, who still live much as they did hundreds of years ago, before the Spaniards came.

These lands, too, have high mountains and thick forests. And like the upper half of South America, they are very hot.

Like South America, their mountain slopes grow coffee; their lowlands grow bananas. In fact, these lands are sometimes called "the banana republics" because of their chief crop.

Mexico is attached to North America, but it is really more like South America. Its people are Indian and Spanish. Its cities are partly new, but many of them look like old Spanish towns. It also has hot, damp forests with banana trees and strange, bright birds and flowers. It has high, jagged mountains with scattered flocks and shepherds. It has tiny, mountain farms and flat plains and deserts.

In the centre of Mexico is a wide, high tableland which has an extremely pleasant climate for the most part of the year.

CENTRAL AMERICA and THE WEST INDIES

GUATEMAL

A village market in Mexico is a busy place.

Central American Indians still have old-fashioned ways of living.

18

There are modern sugar plantations in the West Indies.

There are many bananas grown in Central America.

The islands of the West Indies have some fine harbours.

Huge mahogany trees grow in Central American forests.

Central America has many colourful old Spanish towns.

In Alaska the mountains come right down to the Sea.

The South-west has "forests" of oil derricks.

Great grain elevators hold the wheatlands' harvest.

THIS IS NORTH AMERICA

North America has mountains in the west — the Rockies. It has mountains in the east — the Appalachian chain. And between lie the Great Plains.

North of Mexico, the United States of America reaches across the continent from the Pacific Ocean to the Atlantic. For 1,500 miles from south to north, for nearly 3,000 miles from west to east, you can travel in one country.

Along the Pacific Ocean many fruits are grown. There are oranges in the south, and dates. Farther north come grapes, then apples and pears.

There is fishing along the coast. There are rich oil wells. And ships come and go from great seaports.

NORTH AMERICA

Cowboys practise riding and throwing.

Indians do ceremonial dances in the South-west.

Several mid-western cities have great stockyards.

Busy harbours on the Great lakes ship iron,
copper ore and grain.

Narrow gauge railways carry lumber through the
western forests.

The West has mountains near the coast, in addition to the Rockies. The mountains have gold and silver and many rich stores of other metals. Some mountains are bare of trees and rise up from dry desert lands. Some have fine forests on their slopes, and some of these trees are cut for lumber.

Next come the great cattle ranches. Then the big flat farms, which stretch as far as the eye can see. East of these flat plains the land begins to roll. The farms are smaller, but still fine ones. Many different crops are grown here — cereals, vegetables, food for milk cows and fruit. Dotted among the farms are many small towns for shopping.

More cities appear in the middle of the continent, too. Most of them are built on busy rivers or on one of the Great Lakes. These cities are kept busy shipping goods in and out, and buying and selling. A great many factories are established here, as well, where furniture, tools, clothes, cars, and many other things are made.

21

Modern dairy farms dot the Midwest.

Gold ore is still mined and washed in Alaska.

Cowboys round up cattle on the western range.

Orange groves stretch into the California foothills.

Moving farther east we come to mountains again. These are lower and rounder than those in the West. There is coal in some. There are more forests, especially in the South. And there are swift rivers to provide hydro-electric power for factories. There are iron and steel works and many other factories between these mountains and the Atlantic coast. There are also great cities with millions of people, including New York — one of the largest in the world.

Canada, too, has great mountains and swift rivers and forests for lumbering, in the far West. It also has great wheat plains east of its beautiful Rockies. Canada has rolling land with lakes and smaller farms in the middle part. And more mountains and bigger cities toward the East.

Canada runs right across North America and stretches from the United States far up into the Arctic. But most of its people live in a narrow strip just beyond the United States. North of that strip all is wilderness. There is hunting, fishing, and some mining. But few people live in this rough wooded land or in the cold Arctic wastes beyond.

Alaska stretches out into the Pacific from Canada's western edge. But it is one of the United States. It has great snowy mountains, beautiful lakes, rushing rivers, huge forests, and some small, lively, growing cities.

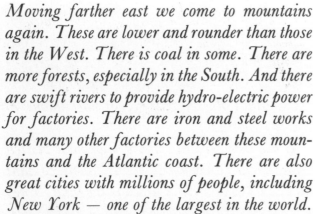

Coal is mined in the eastern United States.

Life is still quiet in villages along the St. Lawrence River.

New York City has the world's tallest buildings.

Fishing is important along the Atlantic coast.

THIS IS ANTARCTICA

Antarctica, beneath its blanket of ice and snow, was the last land on earth to be explored. As recently as 50 years ago, people knew almost nothing about it. No one really makes a home there to this day. For there are only icy winds and snowstorms. No plants grow there. There are few animals to be hunted for food. There are no handy building materials. And it is a very hard place to carry supplies to.

But some men began to wonder about Antarctica. They wanted to know about this frozen land. They wanted to reach the South Pole.

So groups of brave men made plans. They gathered supplies of food and clothing. They hired ships to take them as close as possible to the Pole. They took with them dogs and sleds for transportation on the rest of the journey.

Many of them died on the way. For it was a cold, hard, dangerous trip. But at last one group reached the point which they knew was the South Pole. And they got back home to tell the world.

Since then several other groups have visited Antarctica. They built small towns so that they could stay awhile to study the land. They went about with dog sleds and on snowshoes. They flew over the mountains and over the Pole in airplanes. They made maps and charts. They named mountains and seas. They tested the rocks for mineral riches. Now we know much more than before about this frozen land. Many countries are studying it still.

The last of the continents is Australia. It lies down under the curve of the earth, where the mass of Asia breaks up into bits of land surrounded by water. Many thousands of years ago Australia was probably joined to Asia by a land bridge.

The giant gum trees of Australia seen here are important for timber, oils and dyes.

Australia has animals and plants found nowhere else in the world. Some of them are shown above.

Gold was discovered in Australia about the same time as in the United States. Many new settlers hurried to the country to hunt for gold.

THIS IS AUSTRALIA

Australia is a big, open, uncrowded land. It has some fine modern cities, most of them seaports like Sydney. But beyond the Blue Mountains of the east coast lie the wide open spaces of the continent.

There are fine fields and orchards on the great plains, and bleak mining towns.

Beyond the plains is the wild "bush" country, with scattered sheep stations, as the ranches of Australia are called. In the bush live people called "bushmen" who are different

Australian bushmen like to gather for a dance time called a "corroboree".

Much grain is grown on the Australian plains.

A sheep station on Australia's plains is like a North American cattle ranch.

Rabbits are a great pest in Australia. Fences are built to keep them off the sheep range and out of farms.

from those found in any other country.

Their way of living is very different to that of western countries. But they know the ways of all the animals, and can follow any track through their native bush.

To the north, toward the Equator, are some great, thick forests. But the whole centre of the continent is a desert which is one of the least-known parts of the earth. It is very hot, dry, and hard to travel over. There are parts no man has visited to this day.

The Mediterranean Sea was long the centre of a busy world of trade.

ISLANDS AND SEAS

A piece of land which is surrounded by water but is too small to be a continent is called an island. A large body of water surrounded by land is called a sea or ocean.

The rocky Aleutian Islands, far to the north, border the Bering Sea. They stretch from Alaska, in North America, almost across to the shores of Asia.

The oceans, as you can see on a map of the world, are not surrounded by anything. It is often hard to say where one ends and the next begins. They flow into each other in one great stretch of water at many places.

There are many seas. The one we know best perhaps is the Mediterranean, shown above. Its name means "middle of the world".

As to lakes, they are found in every land. Some of the largest and best-known are the Great Lakes of North America. Africa has huge lakes, too.

Some of the islands of the world are almost as large as seas. The largest are arctic Greenland, and Madagascar, lying close to the eastern coast of Africa.

Many islands, like the British Isles, Japan and the Philippines, are in groups. Let us look at their distinguishing characteristics.

GREAT
BRITAIN

The British Isles are separated from the rest of Europe by the narrow English Channel. They have a mild climate, and much of the land is in farms. But still more than half the food needed, must be brought from outside the islands.

Great Britain has long been a sea power. Many ships are built here, and they travel all over the oceans of the world, trading. Many of her men go to sea, or work in factories which supply the goods those ships carry abroad.

Boating on the River Thames is a favourite pastime in southern England.

Southern England has lovely, rolling countryside.

There are busy factory towns in the north of England.

This is a quiet old English village.

Scotland has rugged highlands.

London is one of the world's great cities.

A shepherd watches his flock above a Scottish loch, or lake.

THE PHILIPPINES

The Philippine Islands are small and mountainous. They are close enough to the Equator to have hot jungles. Many of the trees in these thick forests can be cut down and sold abroad as fine wood. But the light and hollow bamboo is the most popular building material on the islands.

There are great plantations of sugar, rice, tobacco, coffee, and other crops. But most valuable of all is the plant which gives the thread-like hemp. This hemp is made into rope. Many food crops are grown, and there are countless kinds of fish and other seafoods to be had.

Most of the islands of Japan are small and mountainous. The farms often stretch high up on the mountain slopes.

Native homes are built on stilts for protection against floods during the rainy season.

Mountain sides are terraced into small flat fields for growing rice.

Water buffaloes work hard on the farms, and the buffalo cows give milk, too.

Women in the Philippines weave baskets, hats, and fine cloth.

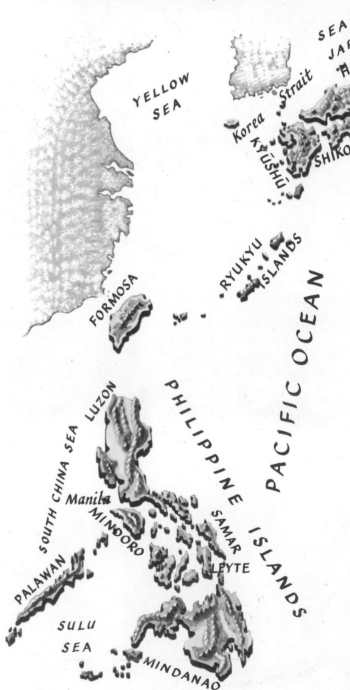

We think of Japan as a part of Asia. Her people belong to the Oriental race, like the Chinese people. And they have many similar ways of doing things.

But the Japanese are cut off from the mainland by water. For many years they also shut themselves away from the rest of the world. They did not want to visit or to be visited by foreigners. They wanted to keep their old ways of doing things.

In modern times, however, they have built factories and schools and have sent some of their young people abroad to other countries to study their ways of living.

Because the Japanese live on islands, many of them are fishermen. They go far from shore in their little boats.

Here is a Japanese house with sliding paper walls.

Japanese gardens are small but beautiful.

Diving for seaweed is a trade in Japan.

The islands of Japan and the thousands of islands that make up the Philippines lie in the western Pacific Ocean. Here ranges of mountains were covered by seas millions of years ago. Now only the mountain peaks show above the surface of the water — as islands.

Women do much of the farm work. Here they are working in the flooded rice fields.

These village people are shown wearing the old-fashioned native costumes of Japan. Today, especially in cities, most people wear Western clothes.

THE EAST INDIES

The East Indies once connected Australia to the continent of Asia. Now most of the land has dropped below the ocean, and only the mountain tops are left.

These islands are rich in woods, oil, gold, silver, and other metals, and in many things that grow.

The weather is hot, but there are welcome breezes, and both plants and animals seem to grow their best on these tropical islands.

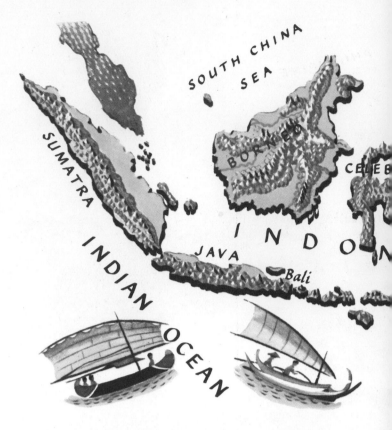

Javanese dancers go to school for long training.

South of the Philippines lie the rich islands of the East Indies.

Houses on Sumatra are built high off the ground.

Music comes from strange instruments in the East Indies, and it sounds strange to western ears, strange but beautiful.

The great plantations of the East Indies were once owned by Europeans.

Temples on the island of Bali have priestesses as well as priests.

OCEANIA

On the Pacific's tiny scattered islands, known as Oceania, live the world's greatest seamen. These handsome, dark-skinned people have no knowledge of science. They have no big ships. But in their hand-made outrigger canoes they can sail for hundreds of miles across the trackless seas.

Their homes and clothing are simple, as in all hot lands. Their wants and needs are simple too. The islands give them fruits to eat. The sea gives them fish for the taking. Once or twice a year trading ships bring supplies from the outside world.

Far out across the Pacific Ocean stretch the tiny dots of land known as Oceania, with hundreds of miles of ocean between.

In these open canoes Polynesian explorers sailed the ocean, settling the scattered islands.

An atoll is a coral island, or a group of them, ringing a quiet lagoon.

Pearl divers lead dangerous lives.

Papeete is the principal city of Tahiti in the Society Islands.

31

Maori women sometimes cook over hot geysers.

Sheep farms cover much of South New Zealand.

Hydro-electric plants provide electricity.

NEW ZEALAND

In the southern part of the Pacific Ocean, near Australia, lie the islands of New Zealand; North and South Islands are the principal ones; Stewart Island lies off the southern coast.

Mountain rivers grace North New Zealand.

There are Maori villages in New Zealand.

New Zealand's islands have beautiful rugged, wooded mountains, great glaciers (which are rivers of ice), snow-capped peaks, and rolling valleys dotted with herds of cattle and sheep.

New Zealand is a pleasant, unhurried place to live. It has a mild climate and good rainfall. The first European settlers found tall, light-skinned, intelligent natives called Maoris living there. There are still many of them to be seen.

SMALLER BODIES OF LAND AND WATER

Can you see a place in a picture below where two bodies of land are joined by a narrow land strip with water on both sides? A strip of land like this has the strange name of isthmus.

This isthmus joins two continents. It connects North and South America. The narrowest part is called the Isthmus of Panama.

A narrow strip of water with land on both sides, joining two larger bodies of water, is called a strait or channel. One strait separates two continents. The Strait of Gibraltar separates Europe from Africa. It connects the Atlantic Ocean with the Mediterranean Sea. The English Channel, between England and France, connects the Atlantic Ocean and the North Sea.

Sometimes a piece of land is almost completely surrounded by water, but is connected to the mainland on one side. This is a peninsula. Look again at the map of Europe on page 8. Boot-shaped Italy is a peninsula, connected to the rest of the continent only at one end. Spain and Portugal together form another peninsula, with sea all around except where they join up with France along the Pyrenees mountains.

A smaller peninsula is a cape.

And what is a body of water called if it is partly surrounded by land? It is known as a gulf or bay. The Gulf of Mexico, for example, is partly surrounded by North America; but on its outer side it flows straight into the Caribbean Sea.

The Isthmus of Panama is a link between North and South America.

The peninsula of Florida borders on the Gulf of Mexico.

The River Seine runs through the lovely city of Paris.

RIVERS

A river, great or small, always has water flowing down a fairly narrow "bed", or channel, toward some sea. Africa has the Nile, which flows four thousand miles through Africa to the Mediterranean Sea. And it has the Congo, which is fed by countless jungle streams on its way to the Atlantic.

South America has the vast Amazon, which winds through trackless jungles

The Congo is a water highway into the jungle.

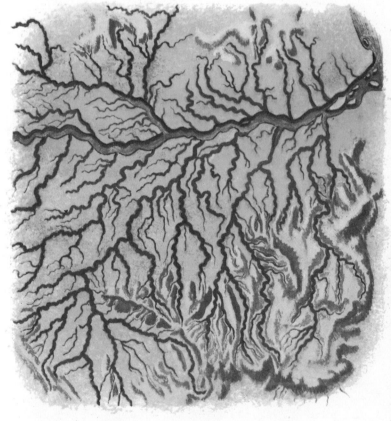

Hundreds of small rivers run into the Amazon.

There are shops and houses, whole little cities, on the river boats of crowded China.

The Danube carries farm goods through Europe from Germany to the Black Sea.

and flows at last into the Atlantic through many wide mouths.

Perhaps the best known river in North America is the Mississippi, which curves its slow way down to the Gulf of Mexico.

Europe has the busy Rhine and Volga, the Rhone and Danube.

Asia has the Indus, the Ganges, and the Yangtze.

And of course every continent has numerous smaller rivers.

The Mississippi River slides along in great, slow curves. A curve like this is called an oxbow because it looks like an ox-yoke.

People come to bathe in the Ganges River in India as a part of their religion.

HIGHLANDS AND LOWLANDS

Every continent has at least one range of mountains which pushes high above the rest of the land. The sharp rocky peaks of some mountains are white with snow all year round.

Mountain slopes are too steep and rocky for farmers to grow crops easily. In some lands farmers build stone walls and make small flat fields called terraces behind them.

Hills stand up above the surrounding country. But they are not as high as mountains. Forests often grow on hills and on the low slopes of mountains.

There are strange flat-topped, steep-sided hills left standing high above the worn-down land around. These are called buttes and mesas.

There are high, flat tablelands called "plateaux" and wide stretches of low, flat land called "plains".

Where there is enough rain and sunshine for grasses and farm crops to grow well, flat land is called "prairie". If it is

plain

butte

pla

grassland

jungle

swamp

steppe

mountain

mesa

hill

canyon

desert

very dry, it is called "desert". If it is too cold for trees and most plants, it is called "tundra". It may be a high windy "steppe". Or a low "jungle" or rain forest, damp and hot, where trees, vines and bushes grow in a thick mat.

The differences are caused by different climates. Now let us see what climate is, and what it means to us.

37

1. Nearness to Poles . . .   or to the Equator.

2. Lots of rain . . .   or almost none.

3. Winds that blow . . .   and storms they cause.

CLIMATE

The kinds of homes and clothes and food people have depend on the climate of the place where they live. Climate is the general kind of weather any place has year after year.

What decides the climate?

1. Nearness to the North or South Pole or to the Equator. (The Equator is the imaginary line running around the earth midway between the poles).

2. How much rain or snow falls.

3. What winds usually blow.

4. How high or low the land is, compared to the level of the sea.

5. How close or far away are seas and oceans. Now let us see what these have to do with the way people live.

5. Nearness to the sea.

The Antarctic is a land of wind and snow and ice. There are no trees, no plants, and only a few animals live there.

Salmon is dried in the short Arctic summer, for winter use.

In winter the husky teams pull heavy sleds long distances over ice and snow.

Greenland's Eskimos raise vegetables in gardens during a short warm season.

LIFE NEAR THE POLES

Around the South Pole is a frozen land called Antarctica. No one at all makes his home there because it is too cold, though some people go for a while to study the land.

A few animals live in the Antarctic — penguins, for example. Seals swim in the cold waters near by.

Great winds blow all the time. There are high snow-covered mountains. But no one ever sees their rocky peaks. For the ice and snow seldom, if ever, melt in the cold Antarctic.

The Arctic is the space around the North Pole. Close to the Pole there are only frozen seas. A little farther away there is bare, treeless land where few plants grow, because of the cold and snow.

The polar bear provides meat and fur.

In summer the Eskimo lives in his earth hut.

The walrus hunt is an exciting adventure.

Eskimos and Laplanders live in the cold, barren lands which surround the Arctic ocean: Alaska, Greenland, northern Canada, Finland and Siberia. They have few kinds of food. They cannot grow fruits or many vegetables. Their work is hunting polar bears, musk oxen, seals, walrus and fish. Meat is their principal food.

For light and heat they burn oil obtained from fish and animal flesh. Fur and animal skins are used for most of their clothing. The skins of animals cover their tiny boats.

In the winter some build homes of blocks of snow; in the summer, of earth. They travel on snowshoes or on flat dog sleds.

It is the icy climate around the North Pole which makes the people there live so differently.

Hunting the ferocious musk ox has its dangers.

Off go the seal hunters in their kayaks.

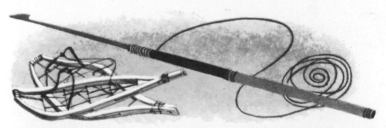

Arctic hunters go on snowshoes and use harpoons.

In winter the Eskimo must travel far for food. He lives then in snow huts called igloos.

Laplanders tend herds of reindeer.

In the hot Amazon valley few clothes are worn by the Indians.

LIFE NEAR THE EQUATOR

Down near the Equator the sun always shines its warmest. The long imaginary line of the Equator runs across Africa, South America, and Indonesia. It crosses the hot damp jungles of the Amazon River valley and the curving Congo River, and dozens of ocean-ringed islands.

In all these places, people live fairly similar lives, because their climates are similar.

Their homes are small and made of clay or grasses or light wood, because people do not need protection from cold, but only from rain and sun. They have almost no furniture, because they spend so much of their time in the open air.

Most months it rains almost every day in the jungle, so trees and vines grow very fast.

In the deep forests of New Guinea live the birds of paradise.

East Africans haul water in calabashes and make bread from the cassava root.

In Borneo many villages are built over the water on stilts.

Their clothes are few, because they do not need to be kept warm. Their skins are dark. Dark skins keep out some of the sun's burning rays.

These people do not need to work very hard to grow food. Crops grow all year round in their gardens. For the land is rich and there is plenty of sunshine and rain. Coconuts and bananas grow on trees without any care at all.

People do not need to work hard for clothes or houses, or for many of the things we need money for in colder lands. Also, when it is so hot all the time, no one has the energy to work very hard. So we do not find many great factories. There is no need for people to live together in cities. They stay spread out in little villages instead. And they live very simply.

Market day is a lively day in a village on Bali.

Fish are abundant in the Pacific Islands.

Palm trees provide leaves for roofs, and fruits to eat; they also give threads for weaving hats and baskets.

LIVING WITHOUT RAIN

To the right are some homes in Africa's great Sahara Desert. They are wide, low tents. Most desert people live in tents or huts of cloth instead of solid houses. This is because the cloth tents are light and easy to move. And desert people must move around very often.

As you see, there are no trees in the open desert. There is only a little grass.

Arabs live in tents in the Sahara Desert.

The tent Arabs on the way to new pastures.

No farm crops will grow without water. So the desert people — in the Sahara, in Arabia, and in Asia's great Gobi Desert — live by raising sheep and goats. The animals quickly eat up all the grass which springs up after short showers. So every few days or weeks the families must roll up their cloth tents, pile all their belongings on to their camels' backs, and find a new place with fresh grass.

Mongols live in felt houses in the Gobi Desert.

Cactus flowers bloom in the deserts of Arizona and New Mexico.

This is an oasis town in the African desert.

Now and then the tent people come to an oasis. An oasis is a place in the desert where underground water comes to the surface. The tent people are glad when they see the tall date palms of an oasis. For there they will probably find a town.

There will be cool houses of mud bricks (for there is no wood or stone in the desert to use in building). There will be gardens and orchards of fruit trees. And there will be a market with small shops where they can buy grain, fruits, salt, and perhaps a new cooking pot. They will sell their wool and meat. Best of all, they will fill their leather bags with water. Then off into the desert they will go again, driving their flocks.

The tent people fill their goat skins with water at the well.

The Arabian Desert yields oil for modern industry.

Shepherds watch their flocks in the Mexican desert. Most desert people are wandering shepherds, because not enough food grows in any one place to feed them, or their flocks, for long.

In many lands seasonal winds bring wet weather —
as shown here — or dry.

The monsoon brings torrential rains

WINDS THAT BLOW

In some lands there are no hot and cold seasons. Instead there are wet and dry seasons. The seasons depend on winds.

"Monsoon" is the name many people give to a wind that blows in from the ocean, bringing rain, at certain times of the year. Farmers plan their crops, and people in towns plan the school year and many other things, according to the monsoons. Let us see how this happens.

Wind is simply moving air. As air grows warmer it grows lighter, and rises. Cool air rushes in below to take its place. And so a wind begins.

In winter, when land is cooler than the ocean, relatively warm air over the ocean rises and cold dry air from the land sweeps out to take its place.

In summer the land is warmer than

A tornado is a violent windstorm covering only a small area. It moves very fast.

the ocean. So the warm air over the land rises. And cooler air from the ocean sweeps in low over the land laden with moisture which comes down as rain, the monsoon rains. Many lands in Asia have these wet and dry winds. So does Mexico.

There are other important kinds of winds on land and sea. On both sides of the Equator there are gentle winds most of the time. They used to blow the great sailing ships which crossed the seas to trade. So they are called "trade winds".

Then there are more violent winds which blow toward the Americas over the Atlantic Ocean. They cause many storms. In winter they bring snow. In summer they bring rain. Sometimes they bring windstorms like tornadoes and hurricanes. Most of the day-to-day changes in our weather are caused by the wind.

A hurricane is a great windstorm covering hundreds of square miles and often lasting a whole day.

RIVERS IN THE SEA

Look at the little island of Iceland. It is a long way north in the Atlantic Ocean. It looks as if it would be freezing cold all year long, doesn't it? Most of it is, too. Most of the high centre of the island is covered with huge fields of ice and snow which never melt. No one lives there.

But Iceland's harbours never freeze over. And the people in its neat, pleasant, though treeless, towns near the coast enjoy fairly mild winters. This is because a current of warm water from the sunny Gulf of Mexico far away, flows up and across the Atlantic Ocean and along the shores of Iceland. It is called the Gulf Stream.

The great winds of the world push the waters of the oceans before them. These streams of water pushed along by the winds are called currents. They affect the climates of the lands they touch. The Gulf Stream is one of these currents.

The warm Gulf Stream keeps Iceland's harbours free from ice though they are near the Arctic Circle.

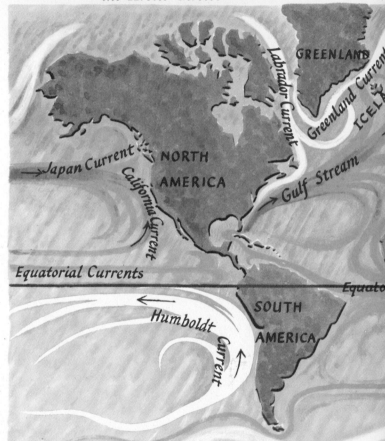

From an aircraft you can see the "river" of the Gulf Stream flowing through the Atlantic Ocean.

48

The warm waters of the Japanese current keep the Japanese Islands from becoming very cold.

An icy Antarctic current makes South America's western coast chilly and bare.

This warm current makes it possible for fishermen to fish all year round near Iceland, and for farmers to raise crops near its shores. The Gulf Stream also influences the climate of Western Europe, including the British Isles.

On the other side of the world, the islands of Japan stretch far north in the Pacific Ocean. But a warm current from the Equator sweeps northward along their shores. And the warm waters bring warm winds which keep the islands from becoming very cold.

There are cold currents, too. Look at the long west coast of South America. Much of the southern coast is cool and bare because a cold current from the icy waters of the Antarctic Ocean sweeps up along those shores.

So "rivers in the sea" change climates in all parts of the world.

49

Villages nestle in the valleys of the Swiss Alps.

UP IN THE MOUNTAINS

Here is a picture of a village high in the mountains. It is a village in the Alps. There are many mountain villages that look something like this, in many different countries. This is because they are all built to suit their climate, high in the mountains.

The air is thinner and colder in the mountains than it is down close to the sea. In the winters there is a good deal of snow. Houses must be sturdily built, with steep roofs, so that the snow will slide off and not form a heavy layer

Mountain men in Afghanistan use yaks to carry heavy loads up steep, rocky trails.

Summer pasture is high in the mountains.

which might crush the house. Most mountain houses are made of wood, because on the lower slopes of mountains there are usually heavy forests of straight, sturdy trees.

Fields for growing crops and feeding animals are small and steep. There are no big farms. Most people keep cows and goats, because these flocks can feed from rough pastures. In the winter they feed on stored-up hay. But in the spring and summer, as the snow melts on the mountainsides, they go up to eat the fresh grass of higher pastures, accompanied by cowherds.

Japanese farmers build up mountain slopes into small, flat terraced fields.

Some Norwegian mountain men work in the forests, cutting trees for lumber in the winters.

Mountain climbers like to climb difficult peaks. They are roped together so that if one starts to fall, the others can hold him up.

Swiss mountain folk do fine wood carving during the long winters.

It is harder to build roads and railways in the mountains than on level ground. So many mountain people seldom go far from home.

Everyone travels on skis in the snowy Swiss winters.

Winters are long and snowy in the mountains. The people of the Swiss Alps keep busy working with their hands, at woodcarving, watch making, embroidery, and other fine crafts.

In Norway the men go fishing or cut wood in the forests. And for the women, there is butter and cheese to make.

Some mountain people learn to travel over the snow on skis. They can slide swiftly down the slopes. Everything in their lives is planned to suit the climate of their country.

Stockholm, in Sweden, is a busy seaport.

DOWN BY THE SHORE

This city is built beside the sea. All around the world there are cities which are like it in some ways because they are on the sea coast.

These are the great seaports of the world. Ships steam into their harbours to unload and collect cargoes at the docks. They steam out from the shelter of the harbour into the open sea, loaded with the goods that country has to sell.

There is always a busy section down beside the water in any port. Long piers push out into the water, with docks or spaces for ships between them.

Often railway tracks run down to the piers or wharfs. Then goods can be quickly loaded and unloaded from trains.

Usually big businesses have warehouses close by, to store some of the goods which travel by water.

Often there are factories in port cities, too. There things are made to be shipped away.

Nearby is the busy centre of the city, with its offices and stores. Then, often up on higher ground, are the homes. Many people have made great fortunes trading by sea. So most port cities have many fine big homes.

This is a typical seaport. See the piers and docks. See the railway tracks. See the warehouses for storing goods. See the factories. See the business section. See the homes beyond.

The lighthouse warns ships at sea of hidden rocks, day and night.

There are many small towns and villages on the sea shores and ocean coasts, too. Most of the families get their living from the sea. Many of the men fish. They go out into the rough seas in small boats, cast their nets into the water, and bring back

Fishing boats vary in size and shape, from trawlers to rowing boats.

A harbour must have sheltered, quiet waters for ships. Some harbours have islands or curving shore-lines to shelter them. Some have man-made sea walls.

their catch to sell. Others are boat builders. Or they pack or can the fish to ship away and sell. Some have shops to sell fishing and ship supplies. One way or another, most of the families in towns along the coast depend for their living on the sea.

Working in a fish cannery is one way to make a living near the sea.

Big ships are built by modern factory methods, but smaller craft are still built in boat yards like this.

There are many fishing villages on the Atlantic coasts. This one is in France.

Many seaside towns are summer re-sorts, where people from far away come to play and rest and swim. For an ocean or sea keeps the weather milder along the shore. The winters are not as cold as they are inland, though winds and storms may be fierce. And the summers are not as hot as in other places. So people from the hot cities like to go to the shore, where breezes are cool.

Sea beaches are pleasant places to go on hot summer days.

The Ohio river, U.S.A.

LIFE ALONG THE RIVERS

A boat whistle hoots. Warning bells clang. Up goes the bridge. And down the river chugs a steamboat trailing flat barges. These barges are the goods trains of our great rivers. They carry coal, food, cattle, all sorts of goods, along the river highways of the world.

Many cities are built along great rivers. Often the banks are walled with stone or brick or concrete to keep the river from washing away bits of the city, or flooding it.

Often cities have parks along the river. But the river banks are busy, too. There are docks where boats load and unload. And often factories are built close to the river.

Some factories use river water in their work; others use the power of the river water to turn wheels to turn machines. Or the water power may be turned into electricity in great plants, and the electricity is then used in factories, as well as in homes.

The Seine in Paris is beautifully lined with trees.

Basel in Switzerland is one of the busiest riverports in Europe.

Where a river flows into the sea, it may deposit sand and soil which builds up small islands.

Many of our great cities are built at the mouths of rivers.

Rivers pass through miles and miles of countryside between the cities and towns.

Where a river runs through a great forest, it may be used in lumbering. Logs are dragged to the river and floated downstream in great loads to the sawmill.

Where small rivers or streams run through woodland or quiet country, fishermen like to camp near the banks to try their luck. They may fish from small boats or from the shore. Or they may wade out into the stream.

There are some rivers along which fishing is done as a big business. In big canneries the fish are prepared for sale. These canneries provide jobs for whole villages of people.

Where rivers run through farmland they are important, too. Often the melting snow on the high land where the

This old-time mill grinds wheat into flour. It uses river water to turn its mill wheel.

Levees are extra walls built up to hold the river in its place when it is running high at flood time.

This factory makes fine leather from animal skins. It uses river water to wash the skins many times.

Trees cut in the forest are brought to ponds like this and are slid into the water. Then they are floated down the river to the sawmill.

river starts fills it to overflowing with water. Then, rushing down through the countryside, the river may overflow its banks and cause a flood.

In some places floods cause great damage. Men keep watch night and day along the banks to see how much the water is rising and to warn people if the water goes too high. They build walls of earth, perhaps with nets of steel for strength, to hold the river in its place.

This big hydro-electric power plant uses the power of river water to make electricity.

Rivers provide pleasant picnic spots in the countryside.

A dam holds back extra river water and lets it through as it is needed. Ditches, called irrigation canals lead river water through the dry fields, so that it nourishes the plants' roots.

Ancient irrigation methods are still being used to water many fields in Egypt.

In other places these floods are eagerly awaited. The yearly flooding of the River Nile keeps bringing new richness to the soil of the Nile Valley in Egypt.

Instead of letting the river waters wash over the land just by chance, men may build dams. These dam walls hold back extra water in great lakes, called reservoirs. Then, little by little, the water is allowed to run through as it is needed. It flows down the river. It flows out into canals. It is led along through the dry country to farms where little rain falls. The river water runs through the fields in ditches and helps the crops to grow.

These dams and supplies of river water are helping to change the climate of some areas. They are changing deserts into rich, fertile farmlands.

INDEX

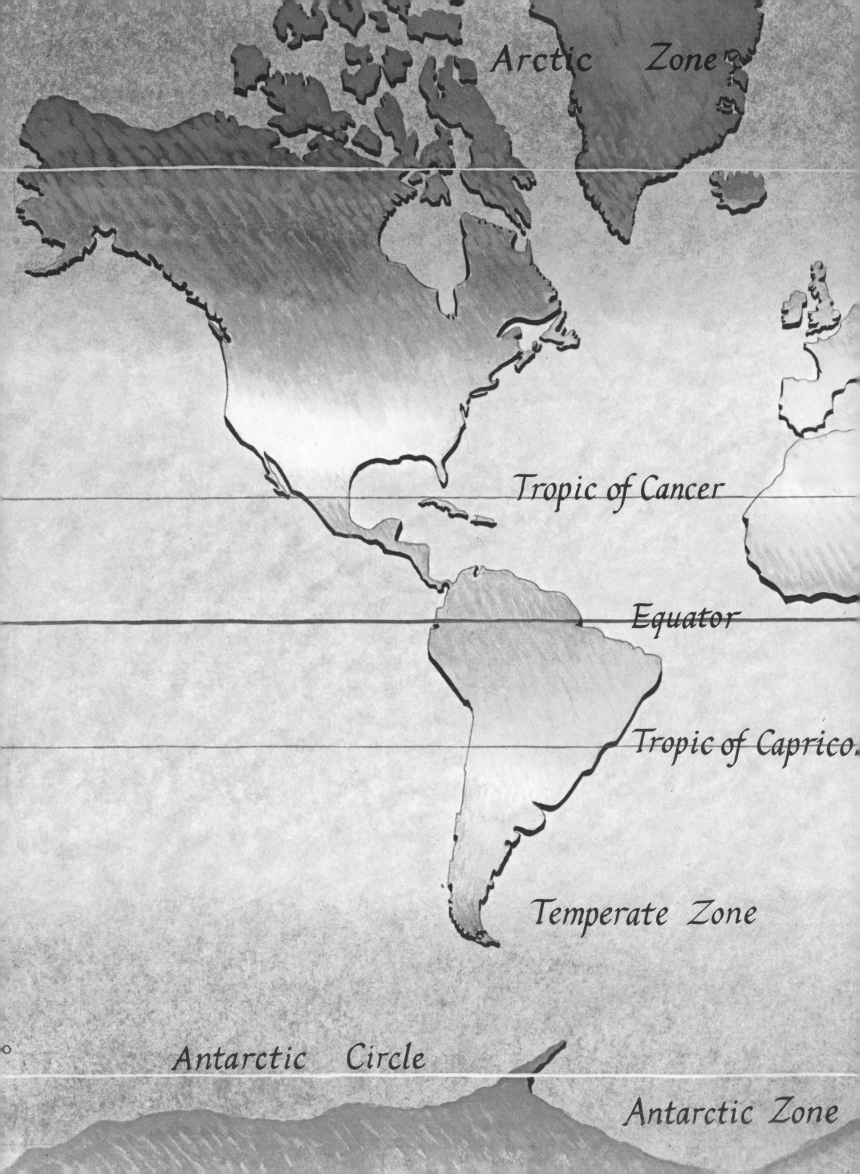